A Grandma Is a Gift from God

EMILIE BARNES

Paintings by DEB STRAIN

HARVEST HOUSE PUBLISHERS

EUGENE, OREGON

A GRANDMA IS A GIFT FROM GOD

Text Copyright © 2004 by Emilie Barnes
Published by Harvest House Publishers
Eugene, Oregon 97402
www.harvesthousepublishers.com

ISBN 0-7369-1103-0

Scripture quotations are taken from the New King James Version. Copyright ©1982 by Thomas Nelson, Inc. Used by permission. All rights reserved.

For more information about other books and products available from Emilie Barnes, please send a self-addressed, stamped envelope to:

> More Hours in My Day
> 2150 Whitestone Drive
> Riverside, CA 92506
> (909) 369-4093

Artwork © by Deb Strain by arrangement with Mosaic Licensing, Inc. It may not be copied or reproduced without permission. For more information regarding artwork featured in this book, please contact:

> Mosaic Licensing, Inc.
> 675 Ygnacio Valley Road, Suite B207
> Walnut Creek, CA 94596
> (925) 934-0889

Design and production by Garborg Design Works, Minneapolis, Minnesota

Printed in China

03 04 05 06 07 08 09 10 11 / IM / 10 9 8 7 6 5 4 3 2 1

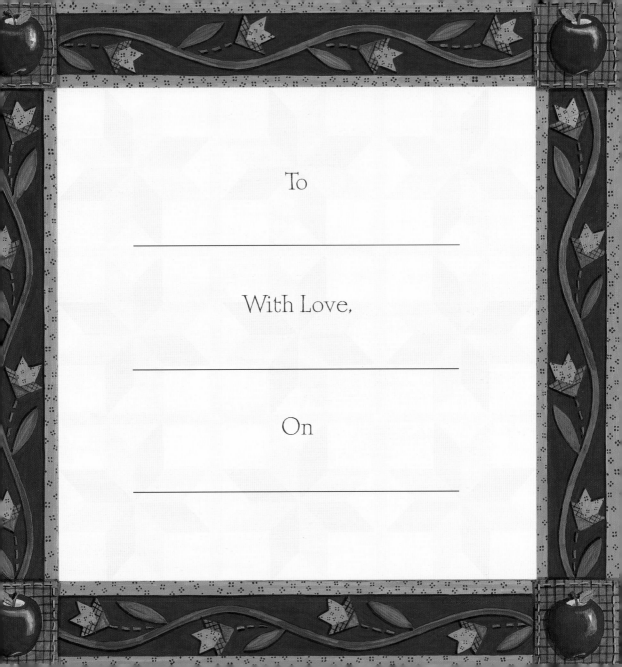

To

_____

With Love,

_____

On

_____

Dedication

I dedicate this book to all grandparents. Without your love, patience, support, encouragement, and modeling, our country would not be the great nation it is today. You are a very valuable part of the American heritage—may this always be true.

I also dedicate this book to all those who took the time to jot down their experiences with their beloved grandparents. Without your real stories this book would not have been possible.

And last but not least, I want to mention the five wonderful grandchildren who light up my life. Without you, my life would not have the purpose and meaning I experience. All of you have given me renewed hope for the future of America. You are wonderful. Thank you for sharing your lives with PaPa and me.

Christine Merrihew
Chad Merrihew
Bevan Merrihew
Brandley Joe Barnes
Weston Barnes

Introduction

Grandmothering means many things to different women, but we all have one thing in common: We have grandchildren. You might be a grandparent of one or ten. The children might live down the street or a great distance away. Some are babies and some are getting into their teenage years. Some are easy to be around and some are at the high-maintenance level.

Some grandmothers may not feel ready; others have been anxiously awaiting the arrival of that first grandchild. But ready or not, here we are. We have arrived at this stage in life which gives us the high calling of grandmothering. We have been fortunate to endure the ups and downs of life to arrive at this sacred throne of honor.

This book has been written to encourage you in this special status. You will find some inspirational memories and stories, bits of wisdom, and godly principles to model with and for these precious possessions.

Whether you are well into the journey or waiting to discover what this journey is all about, jump right in and enjoy this season of your life. You will find it the most exciting and blessed of all your seasons.

The Legacy of Memories

It was an exceptionally warm, sunny day for January in Riverside, California. Two of our five grandchildren were helping my husband and me enjoy this fine day. Ten-year-old Christine was helping me, her Grammy Em, plan and cook dinner. She was picking flowers to arrange for our dinner table. My husband, PaPa Bob as he's called by the grandkids, and Bevan were raking the garden and picking oranges, avocados, and lemons off the trees surrounding our property.

As the afternoon progressed, our working men became hot and tired.

Christine said, "Grammy, let's have tea." That's all it takes for me to stop whatever I'm doing and put the kettle on for Christine and me to have tea! In the process, we poured the men a tall glass of fresh juice on ice and prepared some yummy snacks of toast and jam. We carried the treats up the hill to PaPa and Bevan. How happy they were to receive the refreshment! They thanked us and headed for the bench that sits under a shady avocado tree overlooking the grounds and our quaint, tree-lined little Rumsey Drive which winds by our barn.

As Christine and I headed back toward the house, Christine took my hand and said, "Grammy, I love you."

"I love you too, Christine," I said.

I prepared the teakettle, and Christine pulled down the teapot and put the teacups on

The greatest of these is Love.

the table with our special silver teaspoons. It was an instant tea party.

That night as my Bob and I crawled into bed, we began to share about our day with the wonderful grandchildren.

"What do a PaPa and seven-year-old grandson talk about on the bench under the big avocado tree?" I asked.

"Oh, very special things," Bob replied. "Boys talk just like you girls talk."

I could still picture PaPa Bob and little Bevan—with smudges of dirt on both their faces—sitting on that bench.

Bob continued, "I told Bevan, 'Someday, Bevan, when PaPa's in heaven and you drive down Rumsey Drive as a man, you'll look at this bench we are sitting on, and you will remember the day that Grammy Em and sister Christine served us jam and toast with a glass of juice.' Then Bevan said, 'Not only will I remember, but I will bring my son and someday he will bring his son and point to the bench and tell him about the toast and jam we ate on the bench under the big avocado tree.'"

How does a little boy under-stand and think through the process of generations?

How blessed we are to have these opportunities to teach our grandchildren about the beauty of God's creation, about life and death, and most of all about God Himself.

Take time out of your busy schedule to create a moment to remember forever! Give your time to a grandchild that says, "You are important." All the busyness of life can stop for a short time. These moments are never wasted—you are creating a legacy!

Hopes

9

*Perfect love sometimes does not come
until grandchildren are born.*

WELSH PROVERB

Just a Plain, Old Rolling Pin

My grandmother was raised in an orphanage until she was thirteen, when she went to work as a household servant. She married my immigrant grandfather, himself a widower and father of one small son, at the age of nineteen. She had little formal education to bring into her marriage and very little knowledge of healthy family relationships. What she did bring, however, was a merry laugh and a tried-and-true ability to care for a home, prepare delicious and beautiful meals, and share her gift of baking that is still spoken of by anyone who knew Margaret Sayad.

When my grandfather died, my grandmother moved to my home, bringing all of her worldly possessions with her—and one of these was passed to me. It is a plain, sturdy wooden rolling pin, lacking any particular natural beauty. Yet the worn handles and carved middle are beautiful to me as I remember my grandmother, her kitchen, and all the endless hours she poured into preparing food for those she loved. Every pie I bake brings tears to my eyes as I remember my dear grandmother and her love for God and others.

When this treasure is passed to my daughter, it will be four generations old.

*Donna Otto
Scottsdale, Arizona*

10

Southern Fried Chicken

I think my grandmother was the very best cook that ever lived! As a child I just loved to be invited to have dinner with her. Since she was born and raised in Texas, she really knew how to cook Southern food. My very favorite meal was fried chicken, mashed potatoes, string beans, and biscuits with homemade jam.

From the time I was a little girl Grammy let me help her in the kitchen. I put on an apron, got up on a chair, and assisted her any way I could. My job was to put flour, salt, and pepper in a brown paper bag and mix the ingredients all together. Then I would add a few pieces of chicken in the bag and shake the bag really good. As I would hand the coated pieces to Grammy, she would very carefully place the chicken into an iron skillet. I can still hear the crackling of the chicken as it merged with the grease. This routine would go on until all the chicken was fried with a crispy crust on the chicken.

Grammy had a special way in which she cooked her chicken — she always said it was her secret. After frying all the chicken she would pour off the excess grease, place a little flour in the skillet, mix up the ingredients, add some milk, and make the best white gravy you could ever eat. No one ever made a dinner like my Grammy.

Jenny Whitney
Corona, California

A One Time Feat

I'll never do that again!"

That's what my grandmother said when she finished the Aran-patterned afghan she knitted for me when I was in my early twenties. To my knowledge, she had never done anything like that before. Although everyone in the family had one of her flame-stitch blankets, this bedspread-sized collection of cables, popcorns, and twists was in a class by itself. But she didn't say no when I picked out the pattern.

Instead, she let me choose the wool and then she started to work. Needless to say, it took her a long time to finish. She made it in five long strips then carefully stitched them together. I helped with the elaborate, knotted fringe.

That afghan is still a treasure we use nearly every day. It's warmer than any blanket in the house, and it reminds me whenever I see it of the woman who loved me enough to tackle a daunting task.

And she never did make anything like that afghan again!

Pam Pelliciotti Bailey
Waco, Texas

Therefore be imitators of God as dear children. And walk in love, as Christ also has loved us and given Himself for us, an offering and a sacrifice to God for a sweet-smelling aroma.

EPHESIANS 5:1-2

Being a Grandma

One of the best definitions for grandparent I have ever heard comes from Fitzhugh Downs in his book, *How to Grandparent*: "A grandparent is a unique kind of emotionally involved, part-time parent without pressure."

We are more than a babysitter, we are emotionally involved. We truly care about these young ones who capture our hearts. I like the part about "without pressure"—this season of your life is a joy. It doesn't require all the responsibility of being a parent. When the time comes, we can give our grandkids a hug, a pat on the seat of the pants, and send them home with Mom and Dad. This freedom lets us be more objective in our dealings with our grandchildren. We've done our thing, and now the daily pressures have been reduced. We have the time to talk, take a walk, go fishing, read a book, watch cartoons, take them on vacation.

No matter what your family is like, you will find this a very challenging but rewarding time of your life. Try to let your love flow from you to the lives of your children and their children. Approach this life role as a mature adult with many years of grand experience behind you. Being a grandparent doesn't necessarily come naturally—learn as much as you can about it. Talk to those who have gone before you.

Memories to Cherish

Whoever said, "If I'd known grandparenting was this much fun, I'd have done it first!" certainly had it right. My husband and I enjoy every cherished moment with each of our four grandchildren.

Tradition seems to be the key theme that is central to the relationships that we're developing with each child. One tradition is Sunday night dinners. This, it seems, comes from another era. It's a time when the family gathers around the table and not only eats together but talks until bedtime. If we miss a week, our grandchildren comment, "But we're supposed to be at Nana's."

Birthday celebrations are made very special at Nana's house. The honoree is asked to choose the entire menu, and it's prepared and enjoyed by every family member exactly as requested. Before dessert, each guest is asked to verbally share, as their gift to the birthday child, what they admire about the honoree. These comments of affirmation are so important to each child's development, their positive growth, and their ability to graciously accept compliments.

What grandparenting has become for us, beyond the fun, beyond the individual moments filled with indescribable love for each precious child, is memory building. We create memories for us to cherish as Catherine, Benton, Garrett, and Sam grow older. And we create memories for them to cherish throughout their lives—hopefully passing them on to the next generation, long after we've gone to our eternal home.

Roger and Arlene Garrett
Irvine, California

The righteous shall flourish like a palm tree, he shall grow like a cedar in Lebanon. Those who are planted in the house of the LORD shall flourish in the courts of our God. They shall still bear fruit in old age; they shall be fresh and flourishing.

PSALM 92:12-14

The Passing of Years

Grandmotherhood is a great season of life. Even though our energy level changes and our former opportunities and abilities might change, we are in a great place to share with others what God has graciously prepared us for—the ability to love our family. We no longer have to meet rigid daily schedules. We are now free to set our own priorities and do what's really important.

Scripture presents us with assurances that the aging process is secure in God's hands: our looks, our health, and our circumstances (even though, at times, not to our liking). We may try to stop this process by changing our outward appearances, but real peace comes when we are able to trust how God handles this process. Our mature years define a wonderful time in our lives. We can understand how each day has been ordained by God and trust that there are many blessings still to come. All we have to do is reach out-ward and upward and see what God planned for us even before we were born.

The Gift of Teaching

The original price of 10¢ is stamped on a timeless treasure once owned by my grandmother. I don't know when my grandmother bought her little stainless-steel crochet hook or if it was passed down to her as it was to me. I've often wondered what her thoughts were as she created the dainty gifts for her family and friends with that tiny tool. The many hours of use are still quite evident, as there is a slight curve in the neck of the slender, size 9 hook.

I was not a recipient of any of those beautiful gifts that my grandmother made. Instead of the finished product, I received the tool that was used to make them. It was given to me by my mother. Along with the crochet hook came the joy of learning from her how to use it. My goal was to make a doily. Mom made one right along with me as I learned the stitches, took out rows, and compared progress. She not only taught me the skill that was passed down to her from her mother, but she shared her heart. I learned bits about her childhood that helped me to know her mother, this grandmother who died before I was old enough to remember her. Mother shared a part of herself as she passed along to me the skill and the treasured tool.

I wonder if my grandmother ever thought that her tiny crochet hook would someday belong to her granddaughter along with the joy that she herself must have known as she used it. I'm so thankful for this treasure and the time with my mom. My hope is to pass on this little hook, the skill of using it, and some treasured time to a granddaughter of my own someday.

Connie Taylor
Chehalis, Washington

16

Learning to sew with Grandma
created memories that will last a lifetime.

©Deb Strain

A grandma is old on the outside and young on the inside.

Tim, 7 years old

Christmas Cookies in Grommy's Kitchen

My oldest grandchild, Erik, named me "Grommy" and it stuck. Grommy has a tradition that began with Erik and continues today with the three younger boys—making Christmas cookies in Grommy's kitchen.

We are talking serious baking— rolling the dough, tasting a few samples, making designs with cookie cutters, and taking a peek in the oven to see if the cookies are done. Best of all, this annual event gives me the perfect time to share the Christmas story with the boys.

Now my schedule is full because I am working, but I continue to make the time available especially when the boys say, "Grommy, when are we going to make cookies?"

Such times with our grandkids often lead to discussions about life issues like school, friends, faith, etc.

We never have an agenda except to enjoy our time together. But as grandparents we also want to be on the alert for the opportunity to share the wisdom that life has taught us.

Susan Costa
Mesa, California

The Art of Good Grandparenting

Our goal as grandparents is to bring out the very best in our grandchildren. To be effective, you need to show your grandchildren that you really care for them—not just in words but also in actions. Through their music, friends, clothes, and grades, they are continually asking, "Do you really love me?"

As grandparents we can show we care when we:
- *Really listen.*
- *Take an interest in them as people.*
- *Be clear in our expectations.*
- *Share our knowledge with them.*
- *Reinforce positive behavior and discourage unacceptable behavior.*
- *Trust them to fulfill their promises.*
- *Be flexible and be open to new ideas.*
- *Have a good sense of humor.*
- *Set standards that raise and challenge their standards.*
- *Set the stage for direction of the family unit.*

Remember, you aren't the parent, but you can set the tone for teaching your grandchildren. As the respected grandparent, you are in a very enviable position. The grandchildren love to work along with Grammy and PaPa. You have more influence than you will ever know. Respect that position of praise.

A grammy is jolly, and when she laughs, a warmness spreads over her.

SARAH, 8 YEARS OLD

Tell Me Again…and Again

"I am not a writer, and this is not a book…"

That's how my grandmother began the short memoir she put together for the family several years before she died. She wrote it with a ballpoint pen in her beautiful, legible teacher's handwriting. I then typed it on a word processor (which I was just learning to use) and made copies for her to give as Christmas gifts. My copy, in its simple cardboard binder, is inscribed to me with a "Merry Christmas." I have tucked the original handwritten manuscript inside the cover.

My daughter, Elizabeth, was only three when Mammaw died, and she doesn't really remember her. But I have read my grandmother's little "non-book" to her as a bedtime story. She loved hearing about how her little great-grandma Ella Josephine waded into a creek to escape a spanking, ate roasted sweet potatoes as candy, and talked her way into college at age sixteen. Reading it to my daughter, I was once more impressed by the courage and determination of a little girl who "always wanted to be an explorer."

When my daughter is older, she will have her own copy of her great-grandmother's memoir. She can put it on the shelf with her own treasure…a collection of "Elizabethan sonnets" that her own granddad wrote for her.

Anne Christian Buchanan
Terre Haute, Indiana

Grandmothers are hardly ever cross with you.
And without grandmothers, the world would be a different place.

AVERY, 11 YEARS OLD

Grammy Encouraged Us Along the Way

You can't believe how proud our grandmother Inez Peters was when she came to our grade school to hear that we, her granddaughters Kristia and Kayla, had been nominated for and won the Ambassador Award in our respective grades. This is a very special award for students who show outstanding moral character and leadership qualities for their schoolwork.

Grammy Inez was so humbly proud of us when she heard, "The students that will receive this Ambassador award tonight are truly humble servants of God. They have hearts for their family, friends, and classmates. They never seem to put themselves first. They aren't haughty or arrogant. You see, they have the heart of their Father in Heaven. Their servant's hearts shine through in everything they do. It's as though they do all things as if they are doing them unto the Lord."

These words were pleasing not only to us, but to our parents, and especially to our Grammy Inez. She has added such good qualities to our lives over the years. Without her being in our lives we probably would not have received such a high award. We appreciate our Grammy for all she does for us.

Kristia and Kayla Rusch
Greely, Colorado

Pray Earnestly for Your Grandchildren

No matter if you live near or far away, you can be faithful in daily prayer for your precious grandchildren and for their parents. As children are raised and look back on what kept them on the straight and narrow, they recall the assurance of a praying parent and/or grandparent.

As you talk to the Lord, pray that your grandchildren:

Fear the Lord and serve Him Deuteronomy 6:13.

Know Christ as Savior early in life Psalm 63:1.

Desire the right kind of friends Proverbs 1:10,15.

Will be saved for the right mate 2 Corinthians 6:14.

Submit totally to God James 4:7-8.

Stay protected from wrong people or wrong places Hosea 2:6-7.

Honor their parents Exodus 20:12.

© Deb Strain

Among Angels

One day my five-year-old grandson, Chandler, was playing in my backyard and walked over to my bench that has two yard ornament angels on either side of it. He proceeded to sit down between the angels and said, "Gammie, I know what this bench is for." I was very surprised by what he said next. "This bench is for praying," he explained, "because these angels are praying here and it would be a good place to sit and pray." I was very touched by this. "Out of the mouths of babes"!

Beth Hodge
Plano, Texas

A Spiritual Legacy

My Nana is my spiritual heritage. I spent a lot of time with her as a child because of my parents' divorce, remarriages, and their work schedules. I will never forget the games we played, the television we watched, the stories she told me, and especially the food she cooked for me. But most of all, I remember this small plaque that hung in her home:

> Donde hay fe, hay paz.
> Donde hay paz, hay amor.
> Donde hay amor, está Dios.
> Y donde está Dios, no falta nada.

The translation conveys the meaning if not all the emotion this holds for me: "Where there is faith, there is peace. Where there is peace, there is love. Where there is love, God is there. And where God is, nothing is missing."

Victor Felix Mena, II
Encinitas, California

A Grandparent's Prayer

Please, God,
My children are grown now and I have wonderful grandchildren. I love them all, but please, God, let me remember that I have lived, loved, and enjoyed this life. Do not let me take away from their enjoyment by complaining about every ache and pain. I have earned them all.

Please keep me from mentioning my swollen joints, stiff knees, poor eyesight, and anything else that isn't as good as it once was. Let me remember that I have enjoyed a full and wonderful life and have been blessed in so many ways. Now is not the time for me to begin complaining.

Please let my mouth be closed while my ears are open to hear the fun they are having. Let me remember that I am still setting an example for them and that if I keep quiet, they will forever think that I never had a single ache or pain in my life and that I miraculously escaped the ills of old age.

They will, in later years, remember me with pleasure and say, "I wish I had *her* genes. She never had anything wrong with her!"

That, dear Lord, will be the best legacy I can leave them.

Ann Landers
November 16, 1991

26

To everything there is a season,
a time for every purpose under heaven.

ECCLESIASTES 3:1

The Rewards of Grandmothering

I don't think a gold medal at the Olympics could compare to the rewards I've experienced as a grandmother. Things that got us uptight as a young parent don't seem to stress us out as much. Our gray hair has added layers of wisdom to our thinking process. We have learned to focus on what is really important. We also have more stories to tell and grandpa has more corny jokes.

Here are a few grand rewards and opportunities. I'm sure you can add many more "gold medal" reasons to love being a grandmother.

- The outburst of laughter from uninhibited children is infectious!
- Children tell *great* stories. Write down these precious thoughts and who said them in a journal.
- Savor the times they talk to you about the thrill of being a child. Tell them one of your childhood stories.
- God expresses His love through you to these youngsters.
- Receive renewal for the future by being around the citizens of tomorrow.

© Deb Strain

The Time to Tea

My granddaughter, Christine, and I are kindred spirits. We bonded when she was an infant—my first grandbaby. Our relationship has been special ever since, and tea parties have been part of that special relationship.

One Saturday afternoon as we were walking to the mailbox together, ten-year-old Christine said, "Grammy, let's make some scones and have tea." The next thing I knew, we were in the kitchen whipping up our basic scone recipe. In just a matter of minutes we had popped them in the oven and were setting the table for a simple tea party—just Christine and me.

When the scones were done, we sat down. She poured the tea with practiced ease—we've done this before! We smeared the hot, tasty scones with our favorite jam and whipped topping. But it's what happened next that made the afternoon so special. Once the tea was poured, we began to talk—about friendships, parents, brothers (she has two), and what she could expect as a preadolescent. I was amazed at her knowledge and maturity. We even spoke about spiritual matters—about God and the meaning of life.

What a delightful experience for both of us—just two people who love each other sharing their lives over a cup of tea! We were forty-five years apart in age, yet seconds apart in spirit. I'll never forget that wonderful afternoon.

And it was only later that I realized what had taken place: Christine had asked for a tea party…but she was really asking for *time with me*. It was her way of saying "I need to talk to you."

Jesus Loves Us, This We Know

I have four grandchildren...two boys were born to my son and daughter-in-law and my two granddaughters were adopted from China. These precious girls have brought so much joy to my life. My oldest granddaughter Isabel calls me "My friend, Grammy." She and I are best friends (she is three years old). When I look at this gorgeous, vibrant child who loves to sing and dance and who literally lights up a room when she enters it, I cannot help but be overwhelmed with God's gift to our family.

Her life in a Chinese orphanage would have been grim, but God in His mercy brought her to us. I taught her to sing "Jesus Loves Me" in Chinese when she was two-and-a-half years old. She sings it with gusto, and she knows in her heart how much Jesus and Grammy and Grandpa love her. My lifelong friend, Rosa Bell, taught me to sing that song about 58 years ago.

All of my grandchildren are the greatest gifts I have ever been given. Alex, Nick, Isabel, and our baby Emily light up my life.

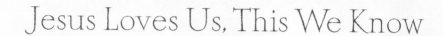

JoJo Bracco
Pflugerville, Texas

*Grandparents do the same things
as parents, only they're nicer.*

KATHERINE, 11 YEARS OLD

How to Be a Good Grandma

If you want your children to welcome you in their lives with open arms, try following some of these ideas:

- *Say positive things to your children about their children.*
- *Never tell your children how to raise their children.*
- *Accept and realize that your children will make mistakes raising their children.*
- *When asked, offer up helpful wisdom…and if it is really good, they may ask again.*
- *When you look after the kids, establish that you will correct them the best way you see fit but with respect for the parents' preferences.*
- *Don't expect your children to appreciate you as you would like to be appreciated.*
- *Be a grandma who reflects love. Be an eternal optimist.*

31

Grandma Gertie's Recipe Book

Ｏne of my favorite and most-used treasures is a little recipe book that my Bob's mother compiled many years ago for my sisters-in-law and me. She wrote down all the recipes our husbands had loved best: main dishes, desserts, jams and jellies — even her famous fried chicken and Texas chili. I have long cherished the generosity of that gift, for she was giving away something she could have kept to herself. She was giving me the power to nurture and cherish her son. In the process she was also giving me a piece of herself.

When I see and use her recipe book it says to me, "Remember Me." She has passed on, but her delicious meals live on. Thanks, Grandma Gertie, for thinking of me!

Celebrations from Afar

My grandchildren live far enough away that I just cannot jump in my car and visit for a day. Jenna is nine and her birthday is early in December. Jacob is twelve and his birthday is in July. Ever since they can remember, I have sent them a "birthday party in a box" and included crackers, cookies, candy, and special surprises like a book, pencils, school supplies, hair clips, etc. for them to share with each other along with their birthday gift. My daughter has often mentioned how much they love it when that box arrives. I always call on their birthday and they, too, tell me how much they enjoy "our party."

E. Margene Curren
Ashtabula, Ohio

A grandmother is a mother who has a second chance.

PAM, 11 YEARS OLD

Memory Makers

As a grandparent we can save the history of our family by doing several things over the years.

- *Preserve your family story and history with photographs.* You can do wonders with digital photography sent via the internet. However, most grandparents have photograph albums. Share these with the children and grandchildren, and instill memories of their heritage.
- *Make an audio and/or video recording of you telling your story.* What a treasure when you're gone.
- *Create individual scrapbooks for each of your grandchildren.* Include photos, notes, bulletins, awards, and letters you have received from them.
- *Write in a diary about your experiences after every grandchild's visit.* These memories will be read by you and loved ones in later years.
- *Save the letters you receive from your children and grandchildren.* These become a great chronological history of your emotions and thoughts.
- *Keep a journal filled with highlights of the day.* You might include who visited, weather, temperature, flowers in bloom, etc.
- *Become a storyteller about your life.* Grandchildren love to hear stories about your youth and the youth of their parents.

Grandma Said...

Hope

Cherish

Give

Wonder

Love

Laugh

Dream

Forgive

Create

© Deb Strain

Threads of love bind
together lasting memories.

36

© Deb Strain

So if you have a grandma,
Thank the good Lord up above,
And give grandma hugs and kisses,
For grandmothers are to love.

LOIS WYSE

Quilted Memories

When my grandmother was eighty years old, she made me a quilt out of material scraps left over from her sewing projects of many years. In the patterns, I could see her aprons, housedresses, curtains, couch slipcover, and my aunt's dresses. She made it with love. It was the first of two she made—the other quilt was for my sister. She said it was something she always wanted to do. She did something new at such an advanced age!

Grandma died at age ninety-eight, a month after my daughter was born. Each time I look at that quilt, I think of who Grandma was, how I loved her and she loved me, and I recall the beautiful creations she made for me, her world, and her home.

Lorraine Lee
Fremont, California

37

© Deb Strain

Long Distance Love

Ever since our granddaughter, Emily, was born, we've discovered a way to help bridge the distance—child-friendly photo albums. I take the photos from a birthday party, Christmas vacation, or any special occasion when we've all been together, and put together a photo book with laminated, decorated pages that the children can handle. These little books can be chewed on, dripped on, and drooled on. And the parents love them too. Everyone in the family has a happy memory of a time together.

Since we don't get to see our grandchildren very often, these photos, that can be looked at and touched whenever they want to, keep us close to them.

And it is "therapy" for me. When I am back home, and my husband and I are missing them so much, we have fun looking at the little photo albums before we send them off.

Dave and Carolyn Alex
Bend, Oregon

© Deb Strain

You shall teach them diligently to your children [grandchildren], and shall talk of them when you sit in your house, when you walk by the way, when you lie down, and when you rise up.

The Wisdom of a Grandma

As grandmothers, we have a wonderful opportunity to share some great godly wisdom with our children and grandchildren. Some of these wisdoms might be:

- *Use your wealth of knowledge.* Tap into your experience to provide wise counsel when needed (Proverbs 1:5).
- *Bridge the gap between parent and child.* Be supportive of your children and their responsibility as parents.
- *Praise God for your long life.* No complaining. Model to your grandchildren that it is okay to grow old and aging can be an enjoyable experience.
- *Be useful and active in the "golden years."* Grandparents have appointments and interests too. Your life is established, so live it (Colossians 2:6-7).
- *Be an example to your grandchildren of forgiveness.* It is the highest form of giving (Ephesians 4:32).
- *Live for today rather than living in the past or dwelling on the future* (Psalm 118:24).

Nobody can do for little children
what grandparents do.
Grandparents sort of sprinkle stardust
over the lives of little children.

ALEX HALEY

The Star and the Heart

When my dreamy, precious granddaughter Kelsey Lee was two years old, sitting between her mommy and daddy at my surprise sixtieth birthday party dinner, I walked by and patted her on her golden curls and whispered in her ear, "You're my star." She turned around, looked at me with those laughing, loving eyes, and replied, "Grammy, you my heart." Since that night, whenever we talk on the phone or send cards and letters, she's been my star and I'm her heart! She will always draw a heart by my name and draw a star by her name. I will always smile at this most treasured tradition.

Shirley Hawkins
Eugene, Oregon

Hot-Buttered Noses

A family tradition that we celebrate on our birthdays is buttering the nose. Each family member gets their nose buttered to "wipe their slates clean"! We never know when the buttering will occur during the celebration, so naturally we are unprepared and our nose as well as half our face gets buttered.

This tradition began with my grandparents and has been carried on by my parents to my sisters and our families. My two-year-old daughter loves this action and wants her nose buttered along with the birthday person. I can remember being at my grandmother's celebrating a birthday and watching her silently signal someone to get the butter. She would rub her finger over her nose a few times until someone caught on.

This is a timeless tradition to me because of the uniqueness and because of the laughter and smiles it brings to our celebrations.

*Sherree Castonguay
Lucerne Valley, California*

41

My Sixteenth Birthday Tea Party

I'll never, never forget when Grammy Em invited me and a few girlfriends over to her house for my sixteenth birthday tea party. I've had many tea parties at Grammy's house before, since I was about four years old, but none were as grand as this one. Grammy let us dress up from her old clothes closet, and we painted ourselves up beautifully with her own makeup. We had so many giggles our sides were sore before we even began our tea.

The tables around the pool area were all decorated with spring colors. As we were seated, our dresses matched the table settings. Grammy had gone all out to make this celebration a memory-maker. My two brothers, Chad and Bevan, were the waiters. They came with their best manners. I was so proud of my girlfriends; they also had their manners stuffed in their pockets. I heard, "yes, please," "no, thank you," "please pass the jam," and "I'd love to."

After eating a hearty meal of scones, butter, jams, dainty sandwiches, and a sweet tart for dessert and before we started to clean up, Grammy announced to all of my guests that the cup and saucer they had been using for the tea was theirs to take home. Grammy had gone to several local antique stores to select special cups and saucers for this occasion. My friends were so thrilled that they could take home something from my very special sixteenth birthday tea party. Grammy truly made a memorable moment for me that day.

Christine Merrihew
Riverside, California

*My grandmother is nice and comfortable
and when she cuddles you,
you can nestle down and feel safe and secure.*

Sadie, 10 years old

Button Treasures

As a special Christmas present last year, my mother decided to stitch buttons from my grandmother's clothes to a card as a memento for me. At the last minute, she added one gray button from my grandfather, too. I love buttons and collect them. They have such stories to tell of days gone by. But more than that, with every button I look at, I see my grandmother in the dresses she wore. My button treasure helps keep her close.

*Nicole M. Tanner
Bellevue, Washington*

Do not pray for gold and jade and precious things;
pray that your children and grandchildren may all be good.

CHINESE PROVERB

A House Full of Memories

I've often said that my ideal home is not one full of new things, but one filled with memories wherever you look.

The secretary from my grandmother's home stirs up the most memories for me. Every time I look at that piece of furniture, I think of her. Family was important to Grammie. She was boarded out for much of her childhood, and she was determined to provide a loving and stable home for her own children. That love and care just kept right on coming to her grandchildren and great-grandchildren, and, I might add, to anyone else who needed a place to stay or a warm meal.

I've often thought how pleased Grammie would be if she could see her secretary now. It holds pictures of four generations of her family, including the great-great granddaughter that she never got to see. The section of the secretary that held Grammie's books is mostly used as her china cabinet was used. On the shelf sit a few cups and saucers, some odds and ends, and a newly purchased child's bunny tea set.

Grammie's secretary reminds me of the special bond that can exist between grandmother and granddaughter. Now, it's my turn to be the grandmother. What a privilege I have to be able to pass on not only Grammie's furniture to future generations, but also her love.

Linda S. Mitchell
Edmonds, Washington

45

©Deb Strain

Grammy Em's Oatmeal Cookies

1 stick (1/2 cup) soft butter (unsalted preferred)
2/3 cup honey
1 egg
1 cup whole-wheat pastry flour
1 teaspoon cinnamon
1/2 teaspoon baking soda
1/2 teaspoon salt
1/4 teaspoon nutmeg
2 cups Quick Quaker Oats, uncooked
1 cup raisins
1 cup carob chips or chocolate chips
1 cup date dices or chopped dates
1 cup chopped walnuts
1 cup coconut, unsweetened (optional) — medium or fine-shredded

Preheat oven to 350°. Grease or spray cookie sheet.

Whisk butter and honey together until well blended and creamy; whisk in egg. Blend dry ingredients in a separate bowl. With mixing spoon stir dry ingredients into liquid ingredients just until evenly mixed. Then mix in evenly the uncooked oats, raisins, chocolate chips, dates, walnuts, and coconut. Drop by tablespoonfuls onto lightly greased cookie sheet, spacing close together. If dough does not hold together well, press each dropped cookie together a bit with fingertips.

Bake for 10-12 minutes. Cool before removing from cookie sheet.

Makes about 4 dozen (5 dozen with coconut).